CW00505103

LJ
10|3|00 ©

Birthdays are a Serious Business

Tudor stories linking with the History
National Curriculum Key Stage 2.

First published in 1996 by Watts Books
96 Leonard Street, London EC2A 4RH
Watts Books Australia 14 Mars Road, Lane
Cove, NSW 2006

© Karen Wallace 1996
The right of Karen Wallace to be identified as
the Author of this Work has been asserted by
her in accordance with the Copyright, Designs
and Patents Act, 1988

Series editor: Paula Borton
Consultant: Joan Blyth
Designed by Kirstie Billingham
A CIP catalogue record for this book
is available from the British Library.
ISBN 0 7496 2235 0
Dewey Classification 942.05
Printed in Great Britain

Birthdays are a Serious Business

by
Karen Wallace

Illustrations by Martin Remphry

W
FRANKLIN WATTS
LONDON • NEW YORK • SYDNEY

For Moley Keane

1

A Mysterious Letter

Arthur Knucklebone stood in the oak-panelled hall of Lockstock Manor. He had been waiting two days to speak to his new master, the Earl of Houndstooth.

Now, those two days seemed like two years. Ever since the Earl of Houndstooth had read the letter delivered by Royal messenger, it was as if Lockstock Manor had been turned upside down.

Arthur chewed thoughtfully on a kidney pie. Maids ran past him with buckets of water dodging servant boys

carrying last year's greasy rushes from the banqueting hall. Housekeepers ran after them. Orders were shouted.

Arthur put his hands over his ears. What on earth was going on?

"Arthur Knucklebone!" boomed a deep voice.

It was the Earl of Houndstooth! Arthur wiped his mouth on his sleeve and opened the heavy oak door in front of him.

The Earl of Houndstooth stood by a huge stone fireplace. He wore an embossed leather jerkin and a silver-

handled dagger hung at his waist. As the door closed, he walked to the window, moving with the soft, purposeful steps of a leopard.

Every time Arthur was alone with the
Earl, his heart started to pound in his chest.
Not that Arthur was afraid, but he knew
he had to be on his guard. He followed the
Earl's gaze out of the window.

A huge barn had appeared on a field
to one side of the house. Arthur was
amazed. Two days ago that field had
been empty.

"Sit down, lad," said the Earl.

Arthur could hardly believe his ears. Sit down? Arthur nearly fell down! No-one was invited to sit down in the Earl's presence! No-one! Not even the important-looking gentlemen on business from London.

"What d'you know about the Queen's court, Arthur?" asked the Earl of Houndstooth.

It was about the last question Arthur expected to hear. Yet, as the noise of hammers and men's voices rattled the windows, he thought of his time as a servant with Sir Francis Drake. He remembered the powerful men from the Queen's court talking late into the night. Arthur remembered the whispered secrets that rose like curls of smoke into the air.

Sir Francis Drake had trusted Arthur and Arthur had never let him down. Perhaps the Earl's question wasn't as strange as it had first appeared.

Arthur knew that Queen Elizabeth I's court was a dangerous place. There were courtiers who were really spies. And spies who pretended to be courtiers.

"Captain Drake has taught you well," said the Earl, smiling. "I am glad he was so fond of my brandy."

Arthur smiled back. One morning, after a night of great and late celebrations at Lockstock Manor, Captain Drake had left Arthur behind by mistake. Not that Arthur was too upset. The Captain had been planning another sea voyage and even though Arthur had been proud to serve him, he was not that keen a sailor. Once round the world had been enough for Arthur Knucklebone.

The Earl looked out the window again. "Everything must be ready," he said.

Arthur's curiosity bubbled over. "Ready for what?" Outside the door, there was a clatter of buckets and the splash of

water on flagstones.

"The Queen is coming to Lockstock Manor," replied the Earl slowly. "The Queen, her court, some two thousand pack horses, four hundred carts and as many people as you would see at a country fair."

Arthur gasped. For the first time, he noticed tents and sheds were sprouting all over the orchard beyond the new barn.

"A visit is always a great honour," said the Earl. "But this time it is also a serious business."

"Why?" asked Arthur.

"On September 7, it is the Queen's birthday," replied the Earl. He fixed Arthur with dark eyes. "And birthdays, especially the Queen's birthdays, are always a serious business."

PLAGUE AND PESTILENCE · · · · · · · ✓
BOILS AND PUSTULES · · · · · · · ·
INFECTIOUS DISEASES · · · · ·

2

Murder in the Air

"Plague and pestilence?" asked a thin man with a pointed face and beady eyes. "Seen any?"

"Certainly not," replied Arthur, stiffly.

"Boils, pustules and infectious diseases?" The man twitched his ratty

moustache. "It's the job of the Royal
Harbinger to ask these things, you know."

"I know," replied Arthur, glumly.
He had just spent the morning with two
Ushers of the Royal Bedchamber. They
had counted and prodded every bed in
the Manor.

The Royal Harbinger opened the lid
of a chest in the corridor and sniffed
meaningfully. "Toilet arrangements?"
he muttered.

"Simply dreadful!" squeaked a man
in rose-pink breeches.

Vivian, Lord Poutworthy, pressed a
scent bottle to his chalky face and breathed
as if it was his last breath on earth.

"And who, sir, are you, sir?" demanded the Royal Harbinger, glaring at Arthur who had just assured him that the toilet arrangements at Lockstock Manor were pretty much the same as anywhere else.

Lord Poutworthy thrust his chin in the air. "I am special envoy to Sir Francis Drake," he replied. "Recently returned from a diplomatic mission in the East Indies."

Arthur could barely believe his ears. He and Lord Poutworthy had been on the same voyage and the only time Lord Poutworthy had left the ship, he had returned in a woven basket rather the worse for wear. In fact, if it hadn't been for Arthur, Lord Poutworthy would never have returned at all.

"How very interesting," replied the Royal Harbinger. "And this young man is your servant, I presume. Tell me, is his word to be trusted?"

Lord Poutworthy snickered. A laugh would have cracked the chalk powder on his face. "Can a servant's word ever be trusted?"

At that moment, the Earl of Houndstooth appeared around the corner. Arthur could tell from the look on his face that he had heard every word.

Lord Poutworthy bowed. The Earl of Houndstooth glared at him. Captain Drake had also forgotten Lord Poutworthy the morning after the great, late celebration. And the Earl was beginning to understand why. Lord Poutworthy was about as useful as a lace handkerchief in a thunderstorm.

"One of the Queen's maids is demanding a special herb to prepare the Queen's face powders," replied the Earl of Houndstooth, curling his lip. "Perhaps

you can give her a few tips." Arthur put his hand over his mouth to hide a smile. Lord Poutworthy shot him a look of pure poison. Then he spun on pointed blue shoes and strutted off down the corridor.

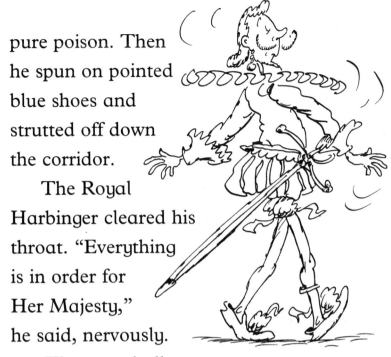

The Royal Harbinger cleared his throat. "Everything is in order for Her Majesty," he said, nervously.

Then we shall wait on Her Majesty's orders, sang a reedy voice.

Now I shall sing a little song.

I wrote it this morning.

It's dull and long.

From inside an oak cupboard came the sound of a lute being played upside down.

The Earl pulled open the cupboard door. A roly-poly man with a wispy white beard fell out in a heap on the floor. He was wearing a long orange hat, and red and green striped clothes.

"Windbag!" bellowed the Earl. "How many times have I told you not to practise in the cupboard."

"But I make up my best songs in the dark," protested Windbag in a squeaky voice. "Songs of life, of love, of luck, of legend." He bowed and the lute banged tunelessly against his knees.

"W-i-n-d-b-a-g," said the Earl of Houndstooth, slowly. "You only sing your songs in the cupboard because that way no-one can hear you and tell you to—"

Windbag held up a red-gloved hand. Mock tears rolled down his cheeks.

He sniffed loudly and without another word, he capered down the corridor.

"If you will excuse me," muttered the Royal Harbinger. "I'm off to count rats."

But the Earl of Houndstooth wasn't listening. "I must do something about Windbag," he said to himself. "The Queen finds jesters boring, these days." He led Arthur into a small room and shut the door behind them.

"The Queen arrives within the hour, Arthur," said the Earl. "And so does an

assassin from the
Spanish Court."

Arthur's face
went white.
"An assassin,"
he repeated stupidly.

The Earl
nodded. "My
informers tell me
he is in disguise."

Arthur tried
to concentrate.
"What can
I do?" he asked.

"There will be dancing and feasting.
There will be hunting and music.
There will be acrobats and
entertainments," replied the Earl. He
paused. "I want you to watch the Queen

and watch who is watching her."

"Me?" squeaked Arthur.

"You," replied the Earl. He drew down his brows over his eyes so that all Arthur could see was his hooked nose and the line of his mouth in his black beard.

"This assassin must be found and found quickly," said the Earl.
"Or heads will roll, Arthur. And those heads will be ours."

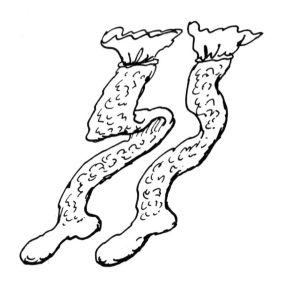

3

Not Enough Marjoram

Queen Elizabeth I sat at her table in the great bedchamber of Lockstock Manor. She sipped at a glass of weak beer and peered at herself in the mirror.

Her skin was still pink from her early morning walk and her brown eyes were bright.

The Queen smiled to herself. Not too big a smile, mind. Her teeth were going black and no amount of white wine, vinegar and boiled honey was making any difference.

There was a rustle of a skirt behind her. "Your preparation is ready, your Majesty," murmured Bessie Codswallop.

"The great Lord Poutworthy did advise me on a new recipe."

The Queen rose and sniffed at a bowl of frothy egg white mixed with borax, poppy seeds and ground up bits of shell. "Not enough marjoram," she said in a testy voice.

Bessie Codswallop pressed her lips together. "My Lord Poutworthy did particularly—"

"I have never heard of a Lord Poutworthy," snapped the Queen.

Anger flushed Bessie's cheeks. Lord Poutworthy had sworn he knew everything about the Queen's cosmetics and he had

particularly advised not to add marjoram.

The Queen whisked out her fan and slapped the back of Bessie's hands. "More marjoram, this minute," she shouted.

Through the open window, Bessie saw Arthur Knucklebone walking in front of the Manor.

"You there," yelled Bessie in a voice as

bad-tempered as that of her mistress.

"Fetch me marjoram from the garden."

"Marjoram?" repeated Arthur.

"You heard," snarled Bessie. "And bring it to the Queen's Bedchamber."

The Queen smiled. Her good humour had returned as she looked at Bessie's plain black and white dress and compared

it to her own richly embroidered yellow
gown. She clapped her hands and three
more ladies-in-waiting appeared. Each
one was carrying a small parcel.

They curtsied. "Good health on your
birthday, Your Grace," they said together.

The Queen ripped open the first
parcel. Two pairs of knitted silk stockings
fell into her hands. "A thousand thanks,
dear ladies," she cried gaily. "I like silk

stockings well."

There was a
knock on the door.

"Who comes to
the Queen's chamber
unannounced?"
bellowed a
lady-in-waiting.

"It is I, Arthur
Knucklebone," cried
Arthur in a jittery voice. "I bring you
marjoram from the garden."

The Queen laughed. "Why should the
lad be so frightened?" she asked. "Surely
his Queen is not such a fearful creature.
Let him come before me."

The ladies-in-waiting were amazed.
It was unheard of for the Queen to see a
servant in her Bedchamber.

The next minute Arthur Knucklebone found himself being dragged towards the Queen's Bedchamber by a determined-looking Bessie Codswallop.

"You must," she snarled. "The Queen commands it."

"I mustn't," protested Arthur, grabbing the leg of a table. "What if she changes her mind?"

But Bessie Codswallop was not

taking no for an answer. She kicked his hand free. "What the Queen wants, the Queen gets," she hissed.

"But it might not be by the time I get there," shouted Arthur.

"Ooh, la, la," said a smooth voice. "What a strange fanciful Queen that would see a servant and not a Count of the French Court."

Bessie Codswallop stopped in her tracks.

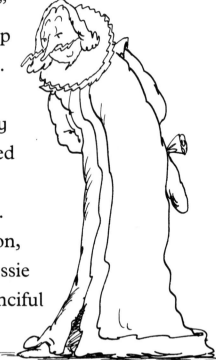

Arthur grabbed the handle of a heavy oak chest. They stared at a tall thin figure, dressed in gold robes.

"I beg your pardon, Count," muttered Bessie Codswallop. "But fanciful or not, those are my orders."

"Of course they are," said the Count, smoothly. "But perhaps you could inform your mistress that the famous fortune-teller, Count Chorizo of Paris, begs an audience." He patted a long narrow pouch at his waist. "I hold the secret to her future."

From behind the Queen's door came an order, "Bessie Codswallop, come here at once." Without a word, Bessie opened the door, went inside and slammed it shut behind her.

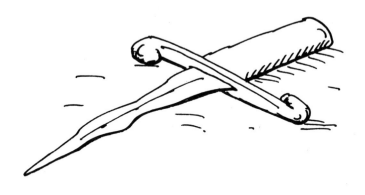

4

What's in a Name?

Arthur Knucklebone ran down the main stairs and out into the open air.

The fields around Lockstock Manor looked like the site of a country fair. Around the side of the house, Arthur could see an endless procession of carts carrying supplies to the great kitchen. In only a minute, he counted two dozen geese, three sheep and one whole ox.

Not that all this fine food would make any difference to Arthur. The chances of it reaching the servants' mouths were next to nothing. In fact, if it wasn't for Phoebe—

"Arthur!" The voice was shy and sweet.

Arthur spun around. A young girl with honey coloured skin and wide green eyes was standing in front of him.

Arthur's heart began to hammer and his tongue felt like a blanket in his mouth.

Phoebe Trewhart worked in the kitchen. She made the best meat pies in the world. And she always kept one for Arthur Knucklebone.

"I-I-" he stuttered.

Phoebe smiled and held out a napkin parcel.

"Steak and onion," she murmured.

Arthur's stomach rumbled as he took an enormous bite. It was the most delicious thing he had ever tasted. He looked sideways at Phoebe. She was the prettiest girl in the world.

"Phoebe," he said.

"Yes, Arthur," cried Phoebe, her honey coloured face going pink at the edges.

Arthur took a deep breath and held her hand in his. "You make the b-b-best pies in the world," he stammered. "Will you—"

"The Queen!" gasped Phoebe, dropping his hand, hitching her skirts and climbing up a pile of rubble to get a better view. "Look, Arthur! The Queen is going to the bear-baiting ring!"

Arthur shook his head at his own stupidity. What on earth was he doing mooning with Phoebe when he was under strict instructions to watch the Queen?

The way down to the bear-baiting ring was clogged with people. Arthur jumped over a hedge and took a muddy short cut that went through the piggery. He came out just behind the huge bear cage that had come all the way from London. In front of the cage stood the Master-of-

Bears, his hand hovering over the latch.
Inside was the biggest, fiercest-looking
bear Arthur had ever seen.

Arthur climbed on top of the cage. The
Queen's special seat was just below him.

At that moment,
the Queen and her
courtiers entered
the ring.

There was
a scramble
as the
Queen took
her seat
and the
Earl sat
down
beside
her.

Arthur felt hugely relieved. If the Earl was there, surely nothing could go wrong. Even so, his eyes wandered over the crowd. Count Chorizo, the fortune-teller, was sitting just out of sight of the Earl.

Arthur stared. What was it that seemed so peculiar about him? Maybe it was the name. He didn't know much about languages but he was sure he had heard *Chorizo* before and it wasn't a French word. Then Arthur remembered an evening with Captain Drake.

Drake had been talking about donkeys, Spanish donkeys. "Poor beasts," he had muttered. "When they're too old to work, the Spaniards turn 'em into sausages. They're called—"

Chorizo. That was the word, Drake had used! All the hairs on Arthur's head

stood up. Since when did a French
fortune-teller have the name of a Spanish
sausage?

At that moment, he saw the Count
lean forward as if he was trying to hide
something. Count Chorizo was drawing a
long glittering blade from his pouch.

Arthur looked desperately at the Earl
of Houndstooth. Somehow he had to warn
him! There was no time to lose!

5

Bessie's Last Stand

Vivian, Lord Poutworthy pressed his bottle of scent to his nose and breathed deeply. Nothing happened.

The stink of sweat, garlic, bears and dung heaps was just as bad as ever. He would have to get another bottle from his

supply up at the Manor. Vivian, Lord
Poutworthy looked at the crowd surging
forward to get a better view. Even the
Queen had left her seat.

Lord Poutworthy preferred monkeys
fighting horses.
Thinking
about
monkeys,
his pale
eyes caught
sight of
a figure
climbing down the side of the bears' cage.

Arthur felt a cold slimy hand wrap
itself round his ankle. The next thing he
knew he was lying on the ground looking
up at the sweat-streaked, chalky face of
Vivian, Lord Poutworthy.

"Ow!" cried Arthur as Lord Poutworthy stamped on his hand.

"That'll teach you not to smirk at your superiors," Lord Poutworthy snarled. "Now fetch me a scent bottle from my chamber."

Arthur opened his mouth, but Lord Poutworthy stuffed a handkerchief in it. Then he grabbed him by the shoulders and spun him in the direction of the big house.

"You take your lying hands off that poor defenceless young man," bellowed

Bessie Codswallop appearing behind him. And without further ado, she thwacked Lord Poutworthy in the stomach with a meaty fist.

Vivian, Lord Poutworthy doubled up in pain and fell to the ground, whimpering. "Try marjoram," sneered Bessie Codswallop. Then she pulled the handkerchief out of Arthur's mouth and grabbed him by the arm.

"Mistress Codswallop!" gasped Arthur. "I have urgent business with the Earl."

Bessie Codswallop grinned at him.

"And I have urgent business with you, Arthur Knucklebone," she cried gaily. She twisted his arm behind his back and shoved him forward. "I want you to show me exactly where the marjoram grows and I do hope it is in a hidden shady place!"

Arthur stared at her in horror. Bessie Codswallop was the last person in the world he wanted to be alone with in a hidden shady place.

He tried to wriggle free but Bessie had a grip like a blacksmith's tongs. "Mistress Codswallop!" shouted Arthur. "The Queen's life is in danger! For pity's sake let me go!"

Bessie Codswallop let out a hoot of laughter. "Ooh, you are a cheeky rascal!" she cried, twisting his arm even further.

They were almost at the huge barn. There was only one thing to do. Arthur didn't like doing it.

He stamped as hard as he could on Bessie's kidskin slippers.

There was a sickening *crunch* and Bessie's grip relaxed.

A mob of people rushed past. The bear-baiting was over. Arthur looked desperately round the bobbing heads. The Queen was nowhere to be seen. Nor for that matter was the Earl of Houndstooth or Count Chorizo.

"Would you like a nut?" asked a man with a monkey on his shoulder.

"I'm looking for the Queen and the Earl," cried Arthur.

"They've gone to the banqueting hall," replied the man popping a grimy nut into his mouth.

Arthur raced up to Lockstock Manor. But the corridor to the banqueting hall was blocked with people.

Arthur ran down the stairs through the kitchen to the other end of the house. There was a small door in front of him.

Arthur took a deep breath and pushed the door open. He found himself standing behind a large screen in the banqueting hall.

6

Arthur Sings for his Supper

Windbag had tried every trick he knew.
He had sung short songs, long songs,
funny songs and sad songs. He had
flattered the Queen. He had danced for
her. He had even done his special back
flips for her.

Elizabeth I sat stony-faced, her thin
lips pulled down at the corners.

Windbag was just about to burst into
tears when he caught sight of Arthur
Knucklebone sneaking into the room.
A brilliant idea occurred to him. He
bowed low in front of the Queen.

And now Your Grace, a little trick.

A handsome lad who's very quick,

Will tell a tale to make you smile.
Come forward, Arthur, I'll cease my
prating,
You mustn't keep our dear Queen
waiting.

A titter went round the room. Even
Arthur smiled to himself. What a mean
trick to play on someone called Arthur.

Then his stomach filled with ice as

Windbag grabbed his wrist and dragged him onto the stage.

A smile flickered on the Queen's face. With a lurch of his ice-filled stomach, Arthur realized she thought his appearance had been specially planned. Windbag slapped his lute into Arthur's hands and without another word, jumped backwards off the stage.

The entire room was silent.

On the Queen's left, sat the Earl of Houndstooth. Beside him was the Count of Chorizo, his hand resting on the pouch at his waist. On the Queen's right sat

Bessie Codswallop and the other
ladies-in-waiting. Vivian, Lord
Poutworthy stood behind.

Suddenly an inspiration
flashed through
Arthur's mind.

This was the
chance he had been
waiting for!

Thrummm! Arthur
played the only chord he knew.

Glad greetings great Queen,
So fair and so true,
Birthdays are a serious business for you.
Your subjects are here with you today,
But one of them is false and should be
Led far away.

Arthur turned to the Earl.

There is a man by your side, dressed

All in gold,
In Spanish, his name means sausage,
I'm told.
He pretends to tell fortunes
But he carries a knife.
Dear Master, I beg you, make use of
Your power!
Arrest this impostor! Lock him up in
the Tower!

The Earl of Houndstooth stared as if he had seen a ghost. Then he pulled out his dagger, pressed it against the Count's heart and led him from the room.

"Bravo!" cried the Queen.

Thrummm!

Arthur grinned at Vivian, Lord
Poutworthy and Bessie Codswallop.

Glad Greetings! great Queen, our
Sun in the sky,
Grant a wish to young lovers
Who would speak but are shy.
Step up, my Lord Poutworthy!
Join hands with your
Bride!
Mistress Codswallop
Stand up!
Take your place
By his side.

Arthur turned
to the Queen.

See before you,
Dear Queen,

True love growing stronger.
Let them be married.
They can tarry no longer!

Lord Poutworthy and Bessie Codswallop stood side by side, glaring at each other like two fighting cats.

The Queen didn't usually approve of her ladies-in-waiting getting married. But she was fed up with Bessie Codswallop ever since she left out the marjoram from her make-up.

The Queen nodded and clapped her hands.

A priest shuffled onto the stage. A moment later Vivian, Lord Poutworthy was married to Bessie Codswallop.

Everyone clapped.

And the Queen clapped louder and longer than anyone else.

Arthur bowed low carefully avoiding the looks of pure hatred coming from the two newly weds. As he stood up, he found himself staring into the Queen's clever eyes.

"A thousand thanks, Arthur," she cried and threw him a purse of gold.

As Arthur caught it, pictures of a new life appeared in front of his eyes.

"Thank you! Your Grace," he cried. Then he ran through the little door all the way back to kitchen.

There was someone he had to speak to. Her name was Phoebe Trewhart and she made the best meat pies in the world!

Queen Elizabeth I

Elizabeth I ruled England
between 1558-1603.

Morning glory

Elizabeth's favourite time of day was the morning.
She liked to go out for an early walk and
afterwards would sit by her window listening to the
conversations below. Then she would have a small
breakfast with weak beer to drink.

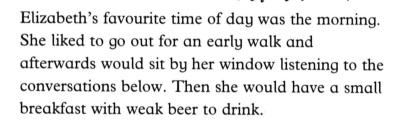

Health and beauty

To keep her face beautiful and
white the Queen would cover it in
a mixture of egg white, alum
borax, poppy seeds and powdered
eggshell. She liked to wear silk
stockings as they helped keep
her warm in the draughty
passages of her palaces.

The Queen's court

The Queen's court was, in many ways, the most important place in the country. Without friends at court and the Queen's support, a nobleman would have little power.

Bear-baiting was a popular sport at the court. The Queen owned a team of prize bears which was looked after by her Master-of-the-Bears.

Jesters, like Windbag, were becoming a thing of the past and the Queen preferred to be entertained by live music and drama.

She was always surrounded by her Maids-of-Honour, but she was very strict with them and wouldn't usually allow them to marry.

The Queen's visits

During the summer, the Queen and her court
travelled around the country to see different people.
These visits were known as 'progresses' and were
considered a great honour although they could
prove to be very expensive for the host. Often when
the Queen's household moved in, the host's
servants had to move out as there was not enough
room for them all!

At one house party, they ate three oxen and
140 geese for Sunday breakfast alone!

Spain and England

Relations were not good between
the two countries during
Elizabeth's reign. There were
many Spanish spies who tried
to enter her court. In 1588, the
Spanish Armada tried to invade
England, but it failed.